The Author's Manual: Navigating the How-To Writing Process

Richard D. Krause

Published by Richard Krause, 2023.

THE AUTHOR'S MANUAL: NAVIGATING THE HOW-TO WRITING PROCESS

First edition. November 12, 2023.

ISBN: 979-8223951704

Written by Richard D. Krause.

Also by Richard D. Krause

The Elderly Trap: Uncovering Scams and Reclaiming Security in the Golden Years.
Ignite Your Motivation and Achieve Your Dreams
The Art of Persoal Mastery: A Roadmap to Success and Fulfillment
The Serenity Solution: Mastering Happiness through Meditation
The Spice Cabinet Apothecary: Natural Health at Your Fingertips
The Author's Manual: Navigating the How-To Writing Process

Table of Contents

Introduction: Unraveling the Mystery of How-To Writing

In the grand tapestry of literature, where words weave intricate patterns and stories unfold like hidden gems, there exists a particular realm that beckons aspiring authors — the enigmatic domain of how-to writing. Have you ever felt the spark of an idea, a whisper of inspiration calling you to share your knowledge with the world? Fear not, fellow wordsmiths, for within the pages of *"The Author's Manual: Navigating the How-To Writing Process,"* we embark on an exhilarating odyssey through the art and craft of crafting impactful how-to books.

The Literary Adventure Begins: A Compass for Aspiring Authors

Imagine, if you will, a vast sea of wordsmithing possibilities stretching out before you like an uncharted ocean. The desire to encapsulate your expertise, your passion, into a tangible creation, a how-to book, is both thrilling and daunting. But fear not, for within the pages of *"The Author's Manual,"* you hold a compass. A trusty guide crafted to navigate you through the exhilarating adventure of transforming your ideas into a literary masterpiece that not only speaks to your soul but captivates your audience.

The Literary Treasure Map: Navigating Uncharted Waters

Consider this manual not just as a book but as a literary treasure map. As you open its pages, you unveil the secrets to selecting a topic that resonates deeply within you while simultaneously capturing the attention of your audience. With your guide in hand, embark on a voyage through uncharted waters, exploring the realms of outlining, writing, and revising. Your manuscript becomes a beacon, a lighthouse of clarity and engagement in the vast sea of literary creation.

Discovering the Power of Your Unique Voice: An Artistic Expedition

But the journey doesn't merely end with crafting sentences; it extends to the very essence of your voice. Picture this: the delicate dance of research, a symphony of visual elements, this manual equips you with the tools to transform your ideas into a compelling how-to masterpiece. It encourages you to uncover the power of your unique voice, guiding you through an artistic expedition where authenticity becomes the brushstroke painting the canvas of your creation.

Beyond the Final Period: Passport to Authorial Realms

Yet, the odyssey doesn't conclude with the final period in your manuscript. ***"The Author's Manual"*** becomes your passport, unlocking the intricate realms of publishing, marketing, and community building. It offers a guiding hand, whether you're contemplating traditional publishing or venturing into the self-publishing frontier. Crafting a killer title, harnessing the magic of social media, the guide is your key to authorship success.

More Than a Guide: A Companion on the Literary Path

This is not just a book; it's a companion on the path to becoming a how-to writing maestro. Join us on this thrilling odyssey, a celebration not just of the act of writing but of the art of connecting with readers. Sprinkled with practical advice, real-life case studies, and a dash of humor, ***"The Author's Manual"*** stands as more than a guide. It is a testament to the transformative power of words, an ode to the joy of crafting stories that resonate.

Turning Literary Dreams into Reality: The World Awaits

Are you ready to turn your literary dreams into reality? Let's embark on this adventure together, pen in hand, imagination alight. The world eagerly awaits your how-to masterpiece. It's time to write it, to share your expertise, to become a guiding light for those seeking knowledge in the vast sea of words.

The Author's Manual: Navigating the How-To Writing Process

Consider this not just a guide but a ticket to unlocking the doors of authorial success. Embrace the journey, dear author, for your readers are waiting. Within the pages of this comprehensive guide, you'll find not only the keys to crafting compelling how-to books but also the inspiration to weave stories that resonate across time and space.

A Literary Call to Arms: Embrace the Journey

In every paragraph, every chapter, hear the call to arms, a rallying cry to embrace the journey, to dive into the depths of your creativity and emerge victorious. Your pen is not just a tool; it's a magic wand, and ***"The Author's Manual"*** is your spell book, guiding you through the enchanting process of creating literary wonders.

So, fellow wordsmiths, let's embark on this literary expedition hand in hand, penning stories that echo through the corridors of time. The adventure awaits, and within the pages of ***"The Author's Manual,"*** the compass is set. Your literary destiny is calling; answer it with a resounding yes!

Chapter 1: Understanding the Landscape of How-To Writing

In the vast literary terrain, where words sprawl like uncharted continents, a peculiar genre stands out - *the how-to book*. Have you ever wondered about the magic behind those step-by-step guides that promise to turn you into a culinary wizard, a DIY master, or a coding guru? Welcome to Chapter 1 of "***The Author's Manual: Navigating the How-To Writing Process,***" where we embark on a journey to unravel the secrets of this fascinating landscape.

Picture this: You're standing at the edge of a literary jungle, filled with a cacophony of ideas, each one vying for your attention. How do you navigate this wild expanse and find your way to the heart of the how-to genre? That's the perplexing puzzle we're here to solve together.

The Evolution of the How-To Genre: A Brief History Lesson

Let's hop into our literary time machine and travel back to the origins of the how-to genre. Imagine dusty scrolls in ancient libraries, filled with instructions on farming, crafting, and perhaps even a guide on how to build a chariot. Fast forward to medieval times, where illuminated manuscripts whispered the secrets of alchemy and potion-making. These early guides were the seeds of what would later become the sprawling forest of how-to literature.

As the world transformed, so did the how-to genre. With the printing press's invention, knowledge became more accessible, and books became the gateway to mastering new skills. The 20th century saw an explosion of how-to books, covering everything from etiquette to space exploration. It was a literary Renaissance, and the how-to genre took center stage.

Reader Expectations: The Shifting Sands

Now, as we stand on the precipice of the 21st century, the landscape has morphed once again. Readers, armed with smartphones and limitless information at their fingertips, crave more than just instructions. They seek engaging narratives, personalized experiences, and a touch of the unexpected.

Today's how-to books are not mere manuals; they are companions on a reader's personal journey. The expectations have shifted from dry instructions to immersive storytelling. Aspiring authors, it's not just about imparting knowledge; it's about crafting an experience that resonates with the reader's soul.

Unveiling the Mystique: What Makes How-To Books Tick?

But what is the allure of the how-to genre? Why do readers flock to these books, hungry for guidance? It's like being drawn to a hidden treasure, and you, dear author, are the mapmaker guiding them through uncharted waters.

Imagine your reader, standing at the crossroads of curiosity and confusion, searching for answers. Your how-to book is the compass that points them in the right direction, the guiding star in their literary night sky. They seek not just information but a trusted companion in their quest for mastery.

The Pioneers: Notable Examples of Successful How-To Books

Before we plunge deeper into this literary adventure, let's pay homage to the trailblazers who paved the way. Think of **"The Joy of Cooking"** by Irma S. Rombauer, a timeless culinary guide that has graced kitchens for generations. Consider **"How to Win Friends and Influence People"** by Dale Carnegie, a manual on human connection that remains relevant decades later. These aren't just books; they are beacons of wisdom that have shaped lives.

As an aspiring author, you're not just joining a genre; you're becoming part of a legacy. Your words have the power to impact, guide, and inspire. The stage is set, and the audience awaits your unique voice in this grand symphony of how-to writing.

The Curious Reader's Dilemma: What draws them in?

Now, let's address the burning question: What draws readers to how-to books in the first place? Is it the promise of newfound skills, the allure of self-improvement, or the simple joy of embarking on a learning adventure?

It's all of the above and more. Readers are drawn to how-to books because they promise transformation. Your book, dear author, is a key that unlocks doors, a ticket to a realm where curiosity meets competence. Whether it's learning to paint, code, cook, or navigate the complexities of life, your how-to book is an invitation to evolve.

The Ever-Changing Landscape: A Call to Adapt

As we wrap up this initial foray into the world of how-to writing, remember this: the landscape is ever-changing. What worked in the past may not be the golden ticket today. Adaptability is your secret weapon. Embrace the challenge, dear author, and let your words be the bridge that spans the gap between confusion and clarity.

In the next chapter, we delve into the heart of your how-to journey: understanding your audience. Like a skilled cartographer mapping unexplored territories, you'll learn to navigate the diverse landscapes of your readers' minds. Ready to unravel the mysteries? Let's embark on this odyssey together, where the compass of ***"The Author's Manual"*** points us towards understanding and connection.

Conclusion:

So here we stand, on the edge of discovery. The how-to genre beckons, and you, dear author, are about to embark on a thrilling adventure. The compass is in your hands, the map unfolding before you. Chapter 1 has laid the groundwork; now, let's journey into the heart of understanding your audience in Chapter 2. The literary odyssey awaits!

Chapter 2: Understanding Your Audience

In the grand theater of writing, understanding your audience is akin to studying the intricate dance of stars in the night sky. Welcome to Chapter 2 of ***"The Author's Manual: Navigating the How-To Writing Process,"*** where we embark on a writing journey to unravel the mysteries of reader connection and tailor your writing to resonate with the hearts and minds of your audience.

Identifying Your Target Audience: Navigating the Writing Crowd

Imagine the vastness of space, each star a potential reader in your literary galaxy. Identifying your target audience is akin to charting constellations, finding patterns among the writing crowd. Who are you writing for? What constellations of interests, needs, and knowledge levels form your readership? This is your writing map, the key to aligning your words with the very essence of your readers.

Analyzing Needs, Interests, and Knowledge Level: Writing Coordinates

As we delve deeper into the writing abyss, let's consider the three essential coordinates: needs, interests, and knowledge level. Your readers, like literary bodies, have unique orbits. What challenges do they face? What sparks their curiosity? Are they beginners navigating a new galaxy of knowledge, or seasoned travelers seeking deeper insights? By understanding these writing coordinates, you align your narrative trajectory with the gravitational pull of your audience.

Tailoring Your Approach: Crafting a Literary Symphony

Picture your writing as a literary symphony resonating across the writing expanse. Tailoring your approach involves choosing the right instruments, the perfect tempo, and the harmonious blend of words that echo in the minds of your readers. Whether it's a soothing lullaby for beginners or a triumphant crescendo for the advanced, your approach crafts the literary soundtrack that accompanies your readers on their writing journey.

The Writing Challenge: Balancing Personal Passion with Audience Alignment

Now, imagine standing at the crossroads of your own passion and the writing needs of your audience. Balancing personal passion with audience alignment is the writing challenge every writer faces. Your passion is the burning star at the center of your creative universe, but to illuminate the paths of others, it must align with the constellations of your readers' interests. It's a dance of writing proportions, where the rhythm of your passion harmonizes with the writing beats of your readers.

Researching and Testing Potential Topics: A Writing Expedition

As we embark on this writing expedition, let's address the quest for the perfect topic. It's like navigating a spacecraft through the cosmos, scanning for cosmic bodies that align with your readers' interests. Research becomes your writing telescope, allowing you to peer into the depths of your reader's preferences. Test potential topics like you would navigate unexplored galaxies, seeking the gravitational pull that captivates your audience.

A Stellar Balancing Act: Personal Passion and Market Demand

The writing dance continues as we explore the delicate balancing act between personal passion and market demand. Imagine your passion as a comet streaking through the writing canvas. While it's essential to follow your passion, consider the gravitational forces of market demand. Are there other stars in the literary sky aligning with your trajectory? A literary equilibrium is achieved when your passion aligns with the writing demand, creating a mesmerizing literary display.

Chapter 2 Navigator's Log: Crafting Your Literary Compass

As we conclude our writing exploration in Chapter 2, consider this your navigator's log—a guide to crafting your Literary compass. Identifying your target audience, analyzing their needs and interests, and tailoring your approach form, the writing coordinates that guide your writing journey. The writing challenge of balancing personal passion with audience alignment becomes your stellar dance, and the research and testing of potential topics propel you through the writing expanse.

The Literary Tapestry Unfurls: What Lies Ahead

The writing challenge may perplex, but within the perplexity lays the beauty of connection. In the chapters ahead, we'll delve deeper into the art of choosing a winning topic, crafting a comprehensive outline, and developing your unique voice. Each step, like a literary body in orbit, contributes to the Literary Tapestry of your writing journey.

So, fellow writing navigators, let the stars guide your pen as we traverse the literary realms of writing. Your audience awaits, and within the pages of *"The Author's Manual,"* the writing map unfolds. Chapter 2 is your Literary Compass; use it to chart a course that resonates across the vast expanse of reader connection. The writing journey continues; let your words illuminate the literary cosmos!

Chapter 3: Choosing a Winning Topic

Welcome, fellow wordsmiths, to the vibrant heart of your literary odyssey! In Chapter 3 of ***"The Author's Manual: Navigating the How-To Writing Process,"*** we embark on a thrilling expedition into the writing realm of topic selection, a journey where the stars align, and your writing finds its orbit.

Strategies for Selecting a Relevant and Marketable How-To Book Topic: Navigating the Writing Sea

Imagine your writing journey as a writing sea, vast and unexplored. The first literary checkpoint is choosing a topic that not only captivates your imagination but also resonates with the beating hearts of your readers. Consider this: What literary bodies light up the writing expanse of your interests? Identify the constellations of your passions, for in their glow lies the guiding light towards a relevant and marketable how-to book.

Strategize like a writing navigator scanning the galactic map. What topics are trending in the literary constellations? Analyze the writing currents, observing which stars in the how-to genre are shining the brightest. Your topic is the literary vessel that will carry readers through the writing adventure you are about to craft.

Balancing Passion with Market Demand: The Literary Conundrum

In this writing ballet, the dance between personal passion and market demand is as intricate as the constellations themselves. Imagine your passion as a writing force, pulling you toward the depths of your creative universe. Yet, the gravitational pull of market demand exerts its influence, guiding you to where readers are eagerly waiting.

Balance becomes your writing conundrum. Navigate this literary equation, ensuring your passion aligns harmoniously with what the writing market desires. The result? A topic that not only fuels your creative spirit but also resonates with the writing currents of reader interest. Let the literary harmony guide your pen.

Researching and Testing Potential Topics: A Writing Laboratory

Now, imagine your writing process as a writing laboratory, a place where you experiment with potential topics like an alchemist seeking the perfect formula. Research becomes your writing microscope, allowing you to delve into the depths of each potential topic, exploring its nuances and hidden facets.

Testing, in this literary laboratory, involves conducting writing experiments, engaging with your potential audience, gauging their reactions, and observing the writing ripples of interest. This phase is your writing voyage, navigating the unknown realms of reader engagement and fine-tuning your topic until it becomes a shining star in your literary galaxy.

The Writing Challenge: Balancing Passion with Market Demand

As you navigate this writing challenge, understand that the balance is not about compromise but about synergy. Picture your passion and market demand as two literary bodies in a writing dance, each influencing the other in a harmonious choreography. Your passion infuses authenticity into your writing, while market demand ensures your words find receptive ears.

Consider the vastness of your potential readership, each star in the writing expanse with unique interests and needs. Your challenge is to find the common threads that tie these diverse writing elements together, creating a tapestry that resonates across the literary universe.

Strategies for Crafting a How-To Book Topic: The Literary Blueprint

Now, let's delve into the strategies for crafting a winning how-to book topic, an intricate process akin to constructing a literary blueprint. Imagine your topic as a writing vessel, charting a course through the how-to galaxy. The first strategy involves tapping into your personal expertise, what writing knowledge do you possess that can illuminate the paths of others?

Next, consider the writing zeitgeist. What topics are currently pulsating through the literary cosmos? Trend analysis becomes your writing telescope, allowing you to peer into the future and select a topic that is not only relevant now but will continue to shine in the writing sky.

As you craft your literary blueprint, think about your potential readers. What writing questions do they seek answers to? What constellations of curiosity do they gaze upon? Your how-to book should be a writing guide, addressing these questions and lighting up the writing pathways for your readers.

Chapter 3 Navigator's Log: Literary Coordinates Set

As we conclude this writing expedition in Chapter 3, consider this your navigator's log, a guide to setting literary coordinates for your writing journey. Choosing a winning topic is your writing North Star, guiding you through the uncharted territories of reader connection and literary success.

Picture your writing vessel poised at the writing dock, fueled by the energy of your passion, aligned with the gravitational pull of market demand. The literary blueprint is your map, and your journey is about to unfold. With topics pulsating like writing energy, let your creativity take flight, and may your words become stars that light up the literary sky.

The Literary Journey Continues: Charting a Course

As we gaze upon the literary cosmos, the journey continues. Chapter 4 awaits, where we delve into crafting a compelling outline, a writing map that guides your readers through the writing expanse of your how-to masterpiece. The literary tapestry of your writing journey is in motion, may your pen be the writing brush painting stories and knowledge across the galaxy. Onward, fellow writing navigators, to the next chapter in our odyssey!

Chapter 4: Crafting a Compelling Outline

Greetings, fellow cosmic explorers! In this chapter of *"The Author's Manual: Navigating the How-To Writing Process,"* we embark on a cosmic journey of a different kind, a journey into the intricate art of crafting a compelling outline. Picture your writing process as a celestial tapestry, and the outline as the cosmic threads that weave your narrative into a masterpiece.

The Importance of a Well-Organized Structure: Cosmic Architecture

Imagine your how-to book as a cosmic structure, standing tall amidst the literary universe. The importance of a well-organized structure is akin to the foundation of a celestial fortress. It ensures stability, clarity, and a seamless flow of energy from the beginning to the end.

Consider your readers as cosmic travelers navigating the intricate corridors of your knowledge. A well-crafted structure becomes their cosmic guide, leading them through the labyrinth of ideas and insights. It is the architecture that transforms your words into a celestial experience.

Building a Detailed Outline: Cosmic Blueprint

Now, picture yourself as an architect of the literary cosmos, sketching the eternal blueprint of your how-to masterpiece. Building a detailed outline is your first stroke on this cosmic canvas. Each section, like a celestial body, has its role, contributing to the overall harmony of your narrative and your cosmic universe.

Your outline is your roadmap, offering a guided tour through the landscapes of your expertise. Think of it as a stellar itinerary, outlining the stops, insights, and discoveries that your readers will encounter. It is not just a roadmap; it's a promise of a wondrous journey that unfolds with precision and purpose.

Incorporating Key Elements for Reader Engagement: Cosmic Alchemy

As you forge ahead with your cosmic outline, consider the alchemy of reader engagement. Imagine your readers as cosmic beings, eager to absorb the subliminal energy of your knowledge. Incorporating key elements becomes your universal elixir, ensuring that each section resonates with your readers and keeps them tethered to your celestial narrative.

These elements can take various forms, captivating anecdotes, thought-provoking questions, or interactive exercises. Picture your outline as a writing carnival, offering readers a thrilling ride through the vast expanse of your expertise. Keep them engaged, and your words become the cosmic attractions they can't resist.

The Cosmic Challenge: Balancing Structure and Flexibility

In the cosmic dance of writing, a challenge emerges: balancing the structured architecture of your outline with the fluidity of creativity. This is where the cosmic challenge lies, to create a framework that guides without stifling, that provides structure without constriction.

Imagine your outline as the stellar orbits of planets. They have a defined path, yet the cosmic forces allow for a graceful dance. Your outline should be flexible, accommodating the unexpected inspirations that may arise during your writing journey. Embrace the challenge, fellow cosmic architects, for it is within this balance that the true literary magic happens.

Chapter 4 Navigator's Log: Writing Navigation Charted

As we conclude our writing journey in Chapter 4, consider this your navigator's log, a guide to charting writing navigation. Crafting a compelling outline is your writing navigation chart, steering you through the cosmic sea of creativity with purpose and clarity.

Your readers, like cosmic travelers, will embark on this journey guided by the map you've crafted. Picture your outline as the North Star, a constant guide in the ever-expanding literary universe. The celestial journey continues, and with a well-crafted outline, your writing vessel is poised for a cosmic adventure.

The Celestial Tapestry Unfurls: What Lies Ahead

As we gaze upon the celestial tapestry, the journey continues. Chapter 5 awaits, where we delve into developing your unique voice—a cosmic resonance that sets your narrative apart. The cosmic threads of your writing journey are being woven, and with each stroke, may your literary masterpiece come closer to fruition. Onward, fellow cosmic architects, to the next chapter in our odyssey!

Chapter 5: Developing Your Unique Literary Voice

Greetings, fellow wordsmiths and literary travelers! In this chapter ***of "The Author's Manual: Navigating the How-To Writing Process,"*** we embark on an enchanting journey into the heart of your narrative, the exploration of your unique literary voice. Picture your writing process as a rich tapestry, and your voice as the vibrant thread that weaves a story uniquely yours.

Finding Your Literary Style: The Symphony of Words

Imagine your literary style as a symphony, a harmonious blend of notes that forms the essence of your narrative. Finding your literary style is like discovering the instruments that resonate with the chords of your creativity. Are you drawn to the eloquence of a violin or the boldness of a trumpet? Your style is the symphonic expression of your literary identity.

Consider this chapter your conductor's baton, guiding you through the rich orchestra of writing styles. Experiment with different instruments, explore various tones, and let your voice resonate like a symphony in the ears of your readers. Your literary style is not just a choice; it's a reflection of your artistic soul.

Balancing Professionalism with Authenticity: The Artistic Tightrope

In the grand circus of writing, balancing professionalism with authenticity is akin to walking a literary tightrope. Picture yourself as the acrobat, navigating the delicate line between formality and personal touch. Your words should be poised, yet authentic; professional, yet infused with the authenticity of your unique literary persona.

Imagine your readers as the audience below, craving a performance that dazzles and resonates. Your literary voice, like the acrobat's movements, should captivate their attention. Strive for a balance that reflects your expertise while inviting readers into the intimate space of your authentic expression. The literary tightrope is a thrilling challenge, but with each step, your voice becomes more refined and captivating.

Connecting with Readers, through Your Voice: The Literary Bond

Now, picture your literary voice as the bridge connecting you with your readers, a bond forged through the resonance of shared experiences. Imagine your words as the bricks in this bridge, each one laid with care and purpose. Connecting with readers through your voice is about creating a literary pathway that beckons them into the world you've crafted.

Consider your readers as fellow travelers, eager to cross the literary bridge you've built. Your voice becomes the guide, offering them a steady hand as they traverse the narrative terrain. Infuse your words with sincerity, and your readers will feel the authenticity in every sentence. A strong literary bond is not just established; it's nurtured through the consistent expression of your unique voice.

The Literary Challenge: Navigating Your Creative Identity

In the labyrinth of literary expression, a challenge emerges, navigating your creative identity. Picture this as a literary quest, a hero's journey into the depths of your artistic soul. The challenge is to unearth the gems of your creativity, to discover the aspects of your voice that make your narrative uniquely yours.

Imagine your creative identity as a treasure map, guiding you through the maze of influences and inspirations. Embrace the challenge, fellow literary explorers, for it is within this quest that you'll uncover the true essence of your writing voice. Your creative identity is a map that, once navigated, will lead you to the literary treasures buried within your soul.

Expressing Your Authentic Literary Self: The Artistic Canvas

Now, let's delve into the art of expressing your authentic literary self, an act as intricate as painting a masterpiece. Imagine your words as brushstrokes, each one adding depth and color to the canvas of your narrative. Expressing your authentic self is about letting the brush dance on the canvas, creating a literary artwork that reflects your true essence.

Consider your narrative as a gallery, and each page as an exhibit showcasing your artistic evolution. Your authentic literary self becomes the curator, selecting the elements that define your narrative style. Don't be afraid to experiment, to let your artistic spirit roam freely on the canvas of your manuscript. The literary canvas is boundless, and your unique voice paints a picture that lingers in the minds of your readers.

Chapter 5 Navigator's Log: Literary Coordinates Set

As we conclude this literary exploration in Chapter 5, consider this your navigator's log, a guide to setting literary coordinates for your writing journey. Developing your unique literary voice is your North Star, guiding you through the vast literary cosmos with authenticity and resonance.

Your readers, like fellow literary travelers, embark on this journey guided by the unique notes of your narrative symphony. Picture your literary voice as the compass, directing your creative ship through uncharted waters. The literary journey continues, and with a well-developed voice, your writing vessel is poised for an odyssey filled with artistic discoveries.

The Literary Tapestry Unfurls: What Lies Ahead

As we gaze upon the literary tapestry, the journey continues. Chapter 6 awaits, where we delve into effective research techniques, a literary excavation that uncovers the gems of knowledge to enrich your narrative. The literary threads of your writing journey are being woven, and with each stroke, may your literary masterpiece come closer to fruition. Onward, fellow literary artisans, to the next chapter in our odyssey!

Chapter 6: Research Techniques - A Literary Excavation

Greetings, fellow literary adventurers! In this chapter of *"The Author's Manual: Navigating the How-To Writing Process,"* we embark on a captivating journey into the art of effective research, an intellectual excavation that unearths the literary gems essential for enriching your narrative. Think of this chapter as your archaeological guide, leading you through the literary terrain in search of knowledge.

Effective Methods for Gathering Information: The Literary Explorer's Toolkit

Imagine your research process as an explorer's toolkit, equipped with tools designed to navigate the vast expanse of information. Effective methods for gathering information are the compass, the binoculars, and the shovel in your literary toolkit. Let's start with the compass, knowing where you're headed is crucial.

Navigate through the labyrinth of information sources with precision. Libraries, academic journals, reputable websites, and interviews with experts become the points on your literary compass. Picture each source as a waypoint, guiding your exploration with accuracy and purpose.

Now, grab your literary binoculars, the art of observation. Skim through books, articles, and online resources with a keen eye. Identify the key concepts, theories, and ideas relevant to your narrative. Your literary binoculars magnify the details, allowing you to spot the gems amidst the vast literary landscape.

Lastly, wield your literary shovel, the tool for digging deep. Delve into primary sources, historical documents, and firsthand accounts. Uncover the layers of information buried beneath the surface. The literary excavation is a meticulous process, requiring patience and a commitment to extracting the authentic jewels that will enrich your narrative.

Evaluating and Citing Sources: The Literary Scholar's Code

Now, imagine yourself as a literary scholar, bound by a code of ethics in the evaluation and citation of sources. As you excavate literary treasures, evaluate each source with discernment. Consider the author's credentials, the publication date, and the reliability of the information. Your literary scholar's code ensures that only the most credible gems find their way into your narrative.

Citing sources is akin to acknowledging the fellow scholars who have paved the way. Picture your citations as nods of respect to those who came before you. Use a consistent citation style, be it APA, MLA, or Chicago, to maintain the integrity of your literary excavation. Let your citations be the signposts guiding readers to the rich intellectual landscape you've explored.

Organizing Research Materials for Easy Reference: The Literary Archivist's System

As you gather your literary treasures, envision yourself as a meticulous archivist, organizing research materials for easy reference. Establish a system, be it digital or physical that allows you to retrieve information effortlessly. Folders, tags, and notes become the filing cabinets in your literary archive.

Consider your research materials as the scrolls in an ancient library. Label them with precision, creating a literary index that mirrors the thematic structure of your narrative. Your organizational system is the key to navigating the vast corridors of information with agility and grace.

The Literary Challenge: Balancing Depth and Relevance

In the literary excavation, a challenge arises, balancing depth and relevance. Picture this as a literary seesaw, where each piece of information carries its weight. Your challenge is to unearth depth without overwhelming your readers and to maintain relevance without sacrificing substance.

Imagine your narrative as a carefully curated museum exhibit. Each artifact serves a purpose, contributing to the overall richness of the display. Prioritize information that enhances the reader's understanding and supports your narrative's thematic arc. The literary challenge lies in finding the perfect balance, a delicate equilibrium that elevates your narrative without drowning it in unnecessary details.

Strategies for Organizing Research Materials: The Literary Maestro's Composition

Now, envision yourself as a literary maestro, orchestrating the composition of your research materials. Employ strategies that transform your information into a harmonious symphony. Begin with a detailed outline, an architectural blueprint that guides the arrangement of your literary instruments.

Think of your research materials as musical notes, each contributing to the melody of your narrative. Arrange them in a logical sequence that flows seamlessly from one point to the next. Create thematic sections, allowing readers to journey through the literary landscape with a sense of coherence and purpose.

Chapter 6 Navigator's Log: Literary Coordinates Set

As we conclude our literary excavation in Chapter 6, consider this your navigator's log, a guide to setting literary coordinates for your writing journey. Research techniques are your North Star, guiding you through the vast literary terrain with precision and purpose.

Your readers, like fellow literary explorers, will embark on this journey guided by the waypoints you've set. Picture your research as the compass, the binoculars, and the shovel in their literary toolkit. The literary journey continues, and with a well-executed research plan, your writing vessel is poised for an odyssey filled with intellectual discoveries.

The Literary Tapestry Unfurls: What Lies Ahead

As we gaze upon the literary tapestry, the journey continues. Chapter 7 awaits, where we delve into writing techniques and strategies, a literary dance that transforms your ideas into a symphony of words. The literary threads of your writing journey are being woven, and with each stroke, may your literary masterpiece come closer to fruition. Onward, fellow literary explorers, to the next chapter in our odyssey!

Chapter 6: Research Techniques - A Literary Excavation

Greetings, fellow wordsmiths and literary enthusiasts! In this chapter of "***The Author's Manual: Navigating the How-To Writing Process,***" we're embarking on an exhilarating journey into the art of effective research, a literary excavation that uncovers the treasures crucial for enriching your narrative. Think of this chapter as your guide through the vast landscape of knowledge, where each discovery is a gem waiting to be polished.

Effective Methods for Gathering Information: Your Literary Explorer's Toolkit

Imagine your research journey as an explorer's toolkit, filled with instruments designed to navigate the vast expanse of information. Effective methods for gathering information are the compass, the binoculars, and the shovel in your literary toolkit. Let's start with the compass, knowing your direction is key.

Navigate the intricate landscape of information with precision. Libraries, academic journals, reliable websites, and expert interviews become the points on your literary compass. Picture each source as a guidepost, steering your exploration with accuracy and purpose.

Now, grab your literary binoculars, the art of observation. Skim through books, articles, and online resources with a discerning eye. Identify key concepts, theories, and ideas relevant to your narrative. Your literary binoculars magnify the details, helping you spot the gems amidst the vast literary landscape.

Lastly, wield your literary shovel, the tool for digging deep. Delve into primary sources, historical documents, and firsthand accounts. Uncover layers of information buried beneath the surface. The literary excavation is a meticulous process, requiring patience and a commitment to extracting the authentic jewels that will enrich your narrative.

Evaluating and Citing Sources: Your Literary Scholar's Code

Now, picture yourself as a literary scholar, bound by a code of ethics in the evaluation and citation of sources. As you excavate literary treasures, evaluate each source with discernment. Consider the author's credentials, the publication date, and the reliability of the information. Your literary scholar's code ensures that only the most credible gems find their way into your narrative.

Citing sources is akin to acknowledging fellow scholars who paved the way. Picture your citations as nods of respect to those who came before you. Use a consistent citation style—be it APA, MLA, or Chicago, to maintain the integrity of your literary excavation. Let your citations be signposts guiding readers to the rich intellectual landscape you've explored.

Organizing Research Materials for Easy Reference: Your Literary Archivist's System

As you gather your literary treasures, envision yourself as a meticulous archivist, organizing research materials for easy reference. Establish a system, be it digital or physical that allows you to retrieve information effortlessly. Folders, tags, and notes become the filing cabinets in your literary archive.

Consider your research materials as scrolls in an ancient library. Label them with precision, creating a literary index that mirrors the thematic structure of your narrative. Your organizational system is the key to navigating the vast corridors of information with agility and grace.

The Literary Challenge: Balancing Depth and Relevance

In the literary excavation, a challenge arises, balancing depth and relevance. Picture this as a seesaw, where each piece of information carries its weight. Your challenge is to unearth depth without overwhelming your readers and to maintain relevance without sacrificing substance.

Imagine your narrative as a carefully curated museum exhibit. Each artifact serves a purpose, contributing to the overall richness of the display. Prioritize information that enhances the reader's understanding and supports your narrative's thematic arc. The literary challenge lies in finding the perfect balance, a delicate equilibrium that elevates your narrative without drowning it in unnecessary details.

Strategies for Organizing Research Materials: Your Literary Maestro's Composition

Now, envision yourself as a literary maestro, orchestrating the composition of your research materials. Employ strategies that transform your information into a harmonious symphony. Begin with a detailed outline, an architectural blueprint that guides the arrangement of your literary instruments.

Think of your research materials as musical notes, each contributing to the melody of your narrative. Arrange them in a logical sequence that flows seamlessly from one point to the next. Create thematic sections, allowing readers to journey through the literary landscape with a sense of coherence and purpose.

Chapter 6 Navigator's Log: Literary Coordinates Set

As we conclude our literary excavation in Chapter 6, consider this your navigator's log, a guide to setting literary coordinates for your writing journey. Research techniques are your North Star, guiding you through the vast literary terrain with precision and purpose.

Your readers, like fellow literary explorers, will embark on this journey guided by the waypoints you've set. Picture your research as the compass, the binoculars, and the shovel in their literary toolkit. The literary journey continues, and with a well-executed research plan, your writing vessel is poised for an odyssey filled with intellectual discoveries.

The Literary Tapestry Unfurls: What Lies Ahead

As we gaze upon the literary tapestry, the journey continues. Chapter 7 awaits, where we delve into writing techniques and strategies, a literary dance that transforms your ideas into a symphony of words. The literary threads of your writing journey are being woven, and with each stroke, may your literary masterpiece come closer to fruition. Onward, fellow literary explorers, to the next chapter in our odyssey!

Chapter 7: Writing Techniques and Strategies - A Literary Dance

Greetings, fellow literary maestros and aspiring scribes! In this chapter of *"The Author's Manual: Navigating the How-To Writing Process,"* we embark on a captivating journey into the heart of crafting compelling narratives, a literary dance that transforms your ideas into a symphony of words. Imagine this chapter as your dance floor, where each word pirouettes and every sentence waltzes to the rhythm of your creative expression.

Tips for Clear and Concise Writing: The Literary Sculptor's Chisel

Picture yourself as a literary sculptor, chiseling away excess to reveal the refined form of your narrative. Tips for clear and concise writing become your chisel, the tool that shapes your words into a masterpiece. Consider each sentence as a sculpted figure, with every word contributing to its clarity and elegance.

Avoid unnecessary embellishments that cloud your narrative like excess marble on a sculpture. Instead, carve out the essence of your ideas with precision. Imagine your readers as art enthusiasts, appreciating the beauty of simplicity in your literary sculpture. Let your words be the chisel strokes that reveal the pure form of your narrative.

Crafting Compelling Introductions and Conclusions: The Literary Entrancer's Spell

Now, envision yourself as a literary entrancer, weaving spells that captivate your readers from the very beginning. Crafting compelling introductions and conclusions becomes your magical incantation, the literary alchemy that sets the tone for your narrative. Think of your opening as the enchanted door, inviting readers into the mystical world you've crafted.

In your introduction, plant the seeds of curiosity. Pose questions, share intriguing anecdotes, or present a thought-provoking scenario. The literary entrancer's spell lies in creating an irresistible allure that compels readers to journey further into your narrative.

Conclude with finesse, leaving your readers with a lingering enchantment. Summarize key points, evoke emotions, or offer a tantalizing glimpse into what lies beyond. The conclusion is your final flourish, the literary spell that ensures your narrative resonates in the minds of your readers long after they've turned the last page.

Using Effective Transitions and Examples: The Literary Navigator's Compass

Imagine yourself as a literary navigator, steering your readers through the narrative seas with seamless transitions. Using effective transitions and examples becomes your compass, the tool that ensures a smooth literary voyage. Consider each transition as a course correction, guiding readers from one idea to the next with clarity and coherence.

Transitions are the bridges that connect your narrative islands. Use words like "furthermore," "however," and "conversely" to create sturdy literary bridges. Picture your readers as explorers, crossing each bridge with anticipation and a sense of direction.

Enhance your narrative with vivid examples that illuminate your ideas. Imagine your examples as beacons, guiding readers through the literary terrain. Whether it's a real-life anecdote, a case study, or a hypothetical scenario, let your examples be the literary constellations that illuminate the path of your narrative.

Creating Engaging Exercises and Activities: The Literary Choreographer's Routine

Now, envision yourself as a literary choreographer, orchestrating routines that engage and delight your readers. Creating engaging exercises and activities becomes your dance routine, the literary choreography that transforms passive readers into active participants. Think of your exercises as dance steps, each one inviting readers to join in the literary dance.

Design practical exercises that allow readers to apply your ideas. Whether it's a thought experiment, a hands-on activity, or a reflection exercise, let your readers waltz through the pages, actively engaging with your narrative. Picture your readers as dance partners, twirling through the literary ballroom you've crafted.

Balance theory with application, ensuring that your exercises reinforce the concepts you've introduced. The literary choreographer's routine is about creating a dance that resonates with readers, leaving them not just informed but also involved in the rhythm of your narrative.

Chapter 7 Navigator's Log: Literary Coordinates Refined

As we conclude our literary dance in Chapter 7, consider this your navigator's log, a guide to refining literary coordinates for your writing journey. Writing techniques and strategies are your North Star, guiding you through the complex dance of narrative creation with finesse and purpose.

Your readers, like dance partners, will twirl through the pages guided by the choreography you've crafted. Imagine your writing techniques as the dance steps, each one leading readers gracefully through the literary ballroom. The literary journey continues, and with a well-executed dance routine, your writing vessel is poised for an odyssey filled with reader engagement.

The Literary Tapestry Unfurls: What Lies Ahead

As we gaze upon the literary tapestry, the journey continues. Chapter 8 awaits, where we explore the integration of visual elements into your narrative, a literary canvas enriched with images, diagrams, and charts. The literary threads of your writing journey are being woven, and with each stroke, may your literary masterpiece come closer to fruition. Onward, fellow literary dancers, to the next chapter in our enchanting odyssey!

Chapter 8: Visual Elements in Literary Creation - A Symphony of Imagination

Greetings, fellow literary architects and visionary wordsmiths! In this chapter of *"The Author's Manual: Navigating the How-To Writing Process,"* we embark on a visually enchanting journey into the integration of visual elements into your narrative, a literary canvas enriched with images, diagrams, and charts. Picture this chapter as your artistic palette, where each visual element adds vibrant hues to your literary masterpiece.

Incorporating Images, Diagrams, and Charts: The Literary Visionary's Brushstrokes

Imagine yourself as a literary visionary, painting a vivid tapestry with the brushstrokes of images, diagrams, and charts. Incorporating visual elements becomes your artistic expression, the tool that transforms your narrative into a captivating work of literary art. Consider each image as a brushstroke, adding depth and color to the canvas of your manuscript.

Images are the visual storytellers in your literary narrative. Whether it's a photograph, illustration, or infographic, let your images speak a thousand words. Imagine your readers as art connoisseurs, appreciating the visual feast you've curated within the pages of your literary creation.

Diagrams are the blueprints that guide readers through intricate concepts. Picture your narrative as a complex architectural structure, and diagrams as the maps that make navigation effortless. Design clear and concise diagrams that enhance understanding and illuminate the literary landscape.

Charts are the rhythmic beats in the symphony of your narrative. Envision your ideas as musical notes, and charts as the notations that bring harmony to your literary composition. Choose the right chart type, whether it's a bar graph, pie chart, or line graph, to convey information with visual clarity.

Working with Designers and Illustrators: The Literary Collaborator's Ballet

Now, envision yourself as a literary collaborator, engaging in a graceful ballet with designers and illustrators. Working with these creative partners becomes your collaborative dance, the choreography that elevates your literary creation to new heights. Think of your designers and illustrators as dance partners, each contributing to the fluidity and grace of your literary ballet.

Communicate your vision clearly, like a dance choreographer guiding the movements of the performers. Share your expectations, themes, and desired tone to ensure a harmonious collaboration. Imagine your literary creation as a stage, and your designers and illustrators as the performers who bring it to life with visual splendor.

Embrace the synergy of words and visuals, allowing each to enhance the other. Picture your readers as the audience, enraptured by the seamless dance of literary expression and visual artistry. The literary collaboration is not just a partnership; it's a dance that captivates the imagination and leaves a lasting impression.

Ensuring Visual Elements Enhance the Literary Content: The Literary Curator's Gallery

As you weave visual elements into your literary tapestry, imagine yourself as a literary curator, meticulously arranging a gallery of visual delights. Ensure that every image, diagram, and chart enhances the literary content, the curation that transforms your manuscript into an immersive experience. Picture your narrative as an art gallery, and each visual element as an exhibit that contributes to the overall aesthetic.

Choose visuals that align with your narrative themes and evoke the desired emotions. Imagine your readers strolling through the gallery of your literary creation, absorbing the visual feast that complements and enriches the written words. Your role as a literary curator is to create a visual narrative that resonates with the audience on a profound level.

Consider the placement of visuals within your narrative, much like arranging artworks in a gallery. Each visual element should flow seamlessly, guiding readers through the literary exhibition with a sense of cohesion. The literary gallery is an invitation to explore, inviting readers to not only read but also visually immerse themselves in the world you've crafted.

Chapter 8 Navigator's Log: Literary Coordinates Illustrated

As we conclude our exploration of visual elements in Chapter 8, consider this your navigator's log, a guide to illustrated literary coordinates for your writing journey. Visual elements are your North Star, guiding you through the creative landscape with a palette of vibrant images, insightful diagrams, and illuminating charts.

Your readers, like gallery visitors, will traverse the visual landscape you've crafted, enraptured by the fusion of words and images. Imagine your visual elements as guideposts, directing readers through the artistic canvas of your literary creation. The literary journey continues, and with a well-illustrated narrative, your writing vessel is poised for an odyssey filled with visual richness.

The Literary Tapestry Unfurls: What Lies Ahead

As we gaze upon the literary tapestry, the journey continues. Chapter 9 awaits, where we delve into drafting and revising your manuscript, a literary refinement that polishes your ideas into a literary gem. The literary threads of your writing journey are being woven, and with each stroke, may your literary masterpiece come closer to fruition. Onward, fellow literary artisans, to the next chapter in our visually captivating odyssey!

Chapter 9: Drafting and Revising Your Manuscript - The Art of Literary Refinement

Greetings, fellow literary architects and masterful wordsmiths! In this chapter ***of "The Author's Manual: Navigating the How-To Writing Process,"*** we delve into the intricacies of drafting and revising your manuscript, a meticulous process that transforms your raw ideas into a refined literary gem. Picture this chapter as your literary atelier, where each word is a brushstroke, and every revision is a step toward perfection.

The Importance of Multiple Drafts: The Literary Sculptor's Workshop

Imagine yourself as a literary sculptor, shaping your narrative with every draft. The importance of multiple drafts becomes your guiding principle—the workshop where your manuscript evolves from a rough concept to a polished masterpiece. Picture each draft as a layer of clay, each iteration refining the contours of your literary sculpture.

Drafting is the raw creation phase, where ideas flow freely like the sculptor's initial strokes. Embrace the chaos of the creative process, allowing your thoughts to manifest without restraint. Picture your readers as art enthusiasts, eagerly waiting the unveiling of your literary sculpture.

Revising is the refining phase, where the sculptor meticulously chisels away excess and hones the details. Imagine each revision as a delicate adjustment, bringing your literary sculpture closer to perfection. Your role as a literary sculptor is to maintain a discerning eye, ensuring that every revision contributes to the overall harmony of your narrative.

Seeking Feedback from Beta Readers: The Literary Collaborator's Circle

Now, envision yourself as a literary collaborator, surrounded by a circle of trusted beta readers. Seeking feedback from these invaluable partners becomes your collaborative circle, the gathering where diverse perspectives shape and refine your literary creation. Think of your beta readers as fellow artisans, each contributing to the collective brilliance of your manuscript.

Share your draft with beta readers who represent different viewpoints, experiences, and expertise. Imagine their feedback as the threads that weave a rich tapestry of insights. Embrace constructive criticism and praise alike, recognizing that each comment is a brushstroke adding depth to your literary canvas.

Engage in open dialogue with your beta readers, much like a roundtable discussion among artists. Picture your manuscript as a living creation, evolving through the collective wisdom of your literary circle. The collaborative circle is not just a feedback session; it's a shared journey toward literary excellence.

Strategies for Self-Editing: The Literary Alchemist's Elixir

As you venture into self-editing, imagine yourself as a literary alchemist, transforming your manuscript into a literary elixir that captivates readers. Strategies for self-editing become your alchemical process, the refining fire that purifies your narrative into a literary potion. Think of your manuscript as raw material and each round of self-editing as a distillation that extracts the essence of your literary vision.

Approach self-editing with a fresh perspective, like an alchemist experimenting with new concoctions. Picture your manuscript as a cauldron, simmering with potential. Identify and eliminate redundancies, tighten sentences, and ensure the flow of ideas is seamless. The literary elixir is crafted through meticulous self-editing, where each correction enhances the potency of your narrative.

Immerse yourself in the language of your manuscript, like an alchemist deciphering ancient texts. Imagine your words as mystical symbols, each holding the key to unlocking the full potential of your literary elixir. The alchemical process of self-editing is both an art and a science, where your manuscript transforms from raw material into a refined literary potion.

Chapter 9 Navigator's Log: Literary Coordinates Refined Again

As we conclude our exploration of drafting and revising in Chapter 9, consider this your navigator's log, a guide to refined literary coordinates for your writing journey. Drafting and revising are your North Star, guiding you through the iterative process with precision and purpose.

Your readers, like patrons of a literary gallery, will appreciate the refined nuances of your manuscript. Picture your multiple drafts, beta reader feedback, and self-edits as the layers that contribute to the depth of your literary creation. The literary journey continues, and with a well-refined manuscript, your writing vessel is poised for an odyssey filled with literary excellence.

The Literary Tapestry Unfurls: What Lies Ahead

As we gaze upon the literary tapestry, the journey continues. Chapter 10 awaits, where we explore the addition of value through case studies, a literary narrative enriched with real-life examples. The literary threads of your writing journey are being woven, and with each stroke, may your literary masterpiece come closer to fruition. Onward, fellow literary artisans, to the next chapter in our refined and meticulously crafted odyssey!

Chapter 10: Adding Value with Case Studies - A Literary Tapestry of Real-Life Narratives

Greetings, fellow storytellers and literary architects! In this chapter of *"The Author's Manual: Navigating the How-To Writing Process,"* we embark on a captivating journey into the world of case studies, a literary narrative enriched with real-life examples. Imagine this chapter as your treasure trove, where each case study is a gem that adds depth and authenticity to your literary tapestry.

Incorporating Real-Life Examples and Case Studies: The Literary Explorer's Expeditions

Picture yourself as a literary explorer, venturing into the rich landscapes of real-life narratives. Incorporating real-life examples and case studies becomes your expedition, the quest for stories that resonate with authenticity and captivate your readers. Think of each case study as a literary artifact, offering insights and lessons that enrich your narrative.

Real-life examples are the beacons that illuminate your literary journey. Imagine each example as a guidepost, showing readers the practical applications of your ideas. Consider your readers as fellow explorers, navigating the literary landscape with the aid of these illuminating tales.

Case studies are the immersive chapters in your literary expedition. Envision your narrative as a grand adventure, and case studies as the vivid stories that unfold along the way. Dive into the depths of real-life scenarios, extracting lessons and weaving them seamlessly into your literary tapestry.

Ensuring Relevance and Relatability: The Literary Conductor's Symphony

Now, envision yourself as a literary conductor, orchestrating a symphony of relevance and relatability within your narrative. Ensuring relevance and relatability becomes your symphonic composition, the harmonious blend of elements that resonate with your readers. Picture each case study as a musical note, contributing to the melody of your literary composition.

Ensure that your case studies align with the themes and objectives of your narrative. Imagine your readers as the audience, attuned to the rhythm of your literary symphony. Select case studies that strike a chord with their experiences, creating a connection that transcends the pages of your manuscript.

Craft case studies that mirror the diversity of your audience. Envision your narrative as a musical ensemble, with each case study representing a unique instrument. Consider the varied perspectives, backgrounds, and challenges of your readers, weaving a tapestry of relatability that resonates across literary boundaries.

Ethical Considerations in Using Case Studies: The Literary Ethicist's Compass

As you navigate the realm of case studies, imagine yourself as a literary ethicist, guided by a moral compass in your narrative choices. Ethical considerations in using case studies become your guiding principles, the compass that ensures integrity and respect in sharing real-life stories. Think of your ethical compass as a north star, keeping your narrative journey true and just.

Seek permission and consent from individuals involved in your case studies. Picture your manuscript as a collaborative venture, where the voices and experiences of those involved are treated with utmost respect. Imagine your readers as witnesses, observing the ethical conduct that underpins your literary creation.

Protect the privacy and confidentiality of individuals within your case studies. Envision your narrative as a sanctuary, where trust is upheld, and personal stories are shared responsibly. The literary ethicist's compass is not just a guide for you but a commitment to treating real-life narratives with the reverence they deserve.

Chapter 10 Navigators' Log: Literary Coordinates Enriched

As we conclude our exploration of case studies in Chapter 10, consider this your navigator's log, a guide to enriched literary coordinates for your writing journey. Case studies are your North Star, guiding you through a landscape of real-life narratives with authenticity and ethical consideration.

Your readers, like co-travelers in this literary expedition, will appreciate the depth and relevance that case studies bring to your narrative. Picture your case studies as milestones, marking the profound moments in your readers' understanding and connection. The literary journey continues, and with a well-crafted tapestry of real-life narratives, your writing vessel is poised for an odyssey filled with reader engagement and enlightenment.

The Literary Tapestry Unfurls: What Lies Ahead

As we gaze upon the literary tapestry, the journey continues. Chapter 11 awaits, where we explore the nuanced art of building credibility as an author, a literary endeavor that establishes your expertise and fosters trust. The literary threads of your writing journey are being woven, and with each stroke, may your literary masterpiece come closer to fruition. Onward, fellow literary artisans, to the next chapter in our intricately crafted odyssey!

Chapter 11: Building Credibility as an Author - The Literary Art of Trust and Expertise

Greetings, esteemed authors and literary artisans! In this chapter of ***"The Author's Manual: Navigating the How-To Writing Process,"*** we embark on a compelling exploration into the nuanced art of building credibility as an author, a literary endeavor that establishes your expertise and fosters trust among your readers. Imagine this chapter as your workshop, where each word is a tool, and every strategy is a brushstroke shaping the portrait of your literary credibility.

Establishing Your Expertise: The Literary Artisan's Masterpiece

Picture yourself as a literary artisan, crafting a masterpiece that showcases your expertise. Establishing your expertise becomes your artistic pursuit, the deliberate strokes that create an impression of authority and knowledge. Imagine your manuscript as a gallery of your literary accomplishments, each page reflecting your commitment to mastery.

Demonstrate a deep understanding of your subject matter, much like a skilled artisan showcasing their mastery of a craft. Consider your readers as discerning critics, appreciating the depth of your expertise woven into the fabric of your narrative. Your role as a literary artisan is to present a canvas that exudes confidence, competence, and a genuine passion for your chosen topic.

Support your claims with evidence and references, like an artisan providing the meticulous details that elevate their creation. Imagine your manuscript as an intricate tapestry, with every citation and reference contributing to the richness of your credibility. The literary artisan's masterpiece is built on a foundation of well-researched facts and a dedication to truth.

Strategies for Building an Author Platform: The Literary Architect's Blueprints

Now, envision yourself as a literary architect, designing the blueprints for a robust author platform. Strategies for building an author platform become your architectural plans, the framework that supports and elevates your literary structure. Think of your author platform as a literary edifice, standing tall and inviting readers to explore the corridors of your expertise.

Develop a strong online presence, much like an architect designing a building that stands out in the skyline. Picture your readers as virtual visitors, navigating the online spaces where your authorial presence is felt. Engage in social media, maintain a professional website, and participate in literary communities to create a platform that reflects your literary identity.

Build relationships with fellow authors and industry influencers, just as an architect collaborates with other professionals in the construction field. Imagine your author platform as a vibrant community, where mutual support and shared wisdom fortify the literary landscape. Your role as a literary architect is to construct a platform that not only showcases your individual brilliance but contributes to the collective strength of the literary community.

Leverage speaking engagements, workshops, and literary events to establish a physical presence in the literary world, much like an architect unveiling their designs to the public. Picture your readers as attendees, absorbing the essence of your expertise in a live setting. The literary architect's blueprints extend beyond the digital realm, reaching into the tangible spaces where your influence as an author takes root.

Leveraging Social Media and Other Platforms: The Literary Ambassador's Networking Gala

As you delve into the realm of social media and other platforms, envision yourself as a literary ambassador hosting a grand networking gala. Leveraging social media and other platforms becomes your diplomatic endeavor, the art of forging connections and spreading your literary influence. Think of each social media post as an invitation, and every interaction as a handshake that leaves an indelible impression.

Choose platforms that align with your literary identity and target audience, just as an ambassador selects events that resonate with their diplomatic mission. Picture your readers as attendees at the gala, mingling in the literary spaces you've curated. Craft engaging content that showcases your expertise, shares valuable insights, and invites readers into the literary conversation.

Engage authentically with your audience, much like an ambassador building genuine connections with diplomats from various nations. Imagine your readers as esteemed guests, appreciating the sincerity and authenticity of your literary diplomacy. Respond to comments, participate in discussions, and cultivate a community where readers feel heard and valued.

Collaborate with influencers and thought leaders, just as an ambassador seeks partnerships to strengthen diplomatic ties. Envision your literary influence as a shared celebration, where the collective voices of authors amplify the impact of the literary conversation. The literary ambassador's networking gala is a dynamic event, constantly evolving and expanding as you navigate the intricate web of social media and other platforms.

Chapter 11 Navigator's Log: Literary Coordinates Fortified

As we conclude our exploration of building credibility in Chapter 11, consider this your navigator's log, a guide to fortified literary coordinates for your writing journey. Building credibility is your North Star, guiding you through the delicate dance of showcasing expertise and fostering trust.

Your readers, like attendees at a literary gala, will appreciate the authenticity and depth that building credibility brings to your narrative. Picture your credibility-building strategies as pillars, supporting the literary edifice you've constructed. The literary journey continues, and with a well-established platform and credible presence, your writing vessel is poised for an odyssey filled with trust and reader connection.

The Literary Tapestry Unfurls: What Lies Ahead

As we gaze upon the literary tapestry, the journey continues. Chapter 12 awaits, where we explore the art of crafting effective titles and subtitles, a literary endeavor that entices readers and encapsulates the essence of your work. The literary threads of your writing journey are being woven, and with each stroke, may your literary masterpiece come closer to fruition. Onward, fellow literary architects, to the next chapter in our intricately designed odyssey!

Chapter 12: Crafting Effective Titles and Subtitles - The Literary Alchemy of Intrigue and Precision

Greetings, esteemed wordsmiths and title-titans! In this chapter *of "The Author's Manual: Navigating the How-To Writing Process,"* we embark on a captivating exploration into the art of crafting effective titles and subtitles, a literary alchemy that weaves intrigue and precision into the very fabric of your work. Picture this chapter as your treasure chest, where each carefully chosen word is a gem that beckons readers into the heart of your literary creation.

Importance of a Compelling Title: The Literary Siren's Call

Imagine yourself as a literary siren, enchanting readers with the melodic call of a compelling title. The importance of a compelling title becomes your siren's song, the irresistible harmony that lures readers into the depths of your literary sea. Picture your manuscript as a vessel, and your title as the ethereal song that echoes across literary waves.

A compelling title is the first impression your work makes on potential readers, much like a siren's call that resonates through the open sea. Consider your readers as sailors navigating the vast ocean of literary options. Craft a title that stands out amidst the literary waves, promising an enchanting voyage into the uncharted waters of your narrative.

Ensure that your title encapsulates the essence of your work, like a siren's song that hints at the mysteries and wonders within. Imagine your readers as captivated sailors drawn by the allure of your literary melody. The literary siren's call is not just an introduction; it's an invitation for readers to embark on a literary journey guided by the harmonious promise of your title.

Creating Subtitles that Clarify and Entice: The Literary Illuminator's Beacon

Now, envision yourself as a literary illuminator, casting a beacon of clarity and enticement through the creation of subtitles. Crafting subtitles that clarify and entice becomes your illuminator's art, the strategic interplay of words that guides readers and sparks their curiosity. Think of your subtitle as a literary lighthouse, beckoning readers to safely navigate the intricate waters of your narrative.

A well-crafted subtitle clarifies the focus and scope of your work, much like a lighthouse that guides ships through treacherous waters. Picture your readers as navigators seeking guidance through the literary sea. Craft a subtitle that acts as a reliable beacon, ensuring readers understand the direction and purpose of your literary voyage.

Infuse your subtitle with an element of intrigue, like a lighthouse that not only guides but also captivates with its luminous allure. Imagine your readers as intrigued sailors, drawn by the promise of discovery hinted at in your subtitle. The literary illuminator's beacon ensures that your work stands out in the vast expanse of literary choices, guiding readers with both clarity and allure.

Considering Marketability and SEO: The Literary Strategist's Chessboard

As you navigate the intricate chessboard of title and subtitle creation, envision yourself as a literary strategist, plotting moves that enhance marketability and visibility through SEO. Considering marketability and SEO becomes your strategic play, the calculated decisions that position your work for success in the ever-evolving landscape of the literary realm. Think of your manuscript as a player on the literary chessboard, and your title as the opening move that sets the tone for the entire game.

Craft a title that is not only captivating but also marketable, much like a chess move that not only captures attention but also secures strategic advantage. Picture your readers as fellow players in the literary game, appreciating the artistry and cunning behind your title choice. A marketable title ensures that your work becomes a strong contender in the vast literary arena.

Infuse SEO-friendly elements into your title and subtitle, like chess pieces strategically positioned for optimal influence. Imagine your readers as digital explorers, navigating the online landscape in search of literary treasures. The literary strategist's chessboard is a terrain where each word is a strategic move, propelling your work toward discoverability and resonance in the competitive realm of online searches.

Chapter 12 Navigator's Log: Literary Coordinates Enchanted

As we conclude our exploration of crafting effective titles and subtitles in Chapter 12, consider this your navigator's log, a guide to enchanted literary coordinates for your writing journey. Titles and subtitles are your North Star, guiding you through the intricate seas of reader engagement and visibility.

Your readers, like eager sailors, will navigate the literary waters with the guidance of your compelling title and illuminating subtitle. Picture your title as a compass, pointing readers toward the literary adventure that awaits them. The literary journey continues, and with a well-crafted title and subtitle, your writing vessel is poised for an odyssey filled with reader intrigue and literary resonance.

The Literary Tapestry Unfurls: What Lies Ahead

As we gaze upon the literary tapestry, the journey continues. Chapter 13 awaits, where we delve into the intricate process of navigating the publishing realm, a literary expedition that explores both traditional and self-publishing options. The literary threads of your writing journey are being woven, and with each stroke, may your literary masterpiece come closer to fruition. Onward, fellow wordsmiths, to the next chapter in our intricately designed odyssey!

Chapter 13: Navigating the Publishing Process - Literary Voyages into Traditional and Self-Publishing Realms

Ahoy, fellow navigators of the written word! In this chapter of *"The Author's Manual: Navigating the How-To Writing Process,"* we set sail on a thrilling literary expedition into the vast seas of the publishing realm. Picture this chapter as your trusty compass, guiding you through the diverse waters of both traditional and self-publishing options, a voyage where each decision shapes the destiny of your literary creation.

Overview of Traditional and Self-Publishing Options: The Literary Cartographer's Map

Imagine yourself as a literary cartographer, sketching the contours of your publishing journey on a map that unfolds possibilities. An overview of traditional and self-publishing options becomes your map—the visual guide that illuminates the distinct landscapes and potential routes your manuscript can traverse. Picture your readers as fellow explorers, peering over the edge of the literary map with anticipation.

Traditional publishing is the well-trodden path, much like an established trade route that promises the guidance of experienced hands. Envision your manuscript as a cargo ship carrying literary treasures, ready to embark on a journey under the banner of a traditional publishing house. Traditional publishing offers the allure of validation and broad distribution, with the potential for your literary cargo to reach the hands of readers around the world.

Self-publishing is the uncharted territory, reminiscent of a daring expedition into the unknown. Picture your manuscript as an intrepid explorer, equipped with the tools of self-publishing and navigating the literary landscape independently. Self-publishing offers the freedom to chart your own course, control your timeline, and retain a lion's share of the literary spoils.

Steps Involved in Getting Your Book Published: The Literary Captain's Log

Now, envision yourself as a literary captain, steering your manuscript through the various stages involved in getting it published. The steps involved in getting your book published become your captain's log, the detailed record of your publishing odyssey. Think of your manuscript as a sturdy vessel, and each step as a nautical mile that brings you closer to the shores of literary fulfillment.

Prepare your manuscript for submission, much like a captain ensuring their ship is seaworthy before embarking on a grand voyage. Imagine literary agents and editors as discerning harbor masters, reviewing your manuscript and granting permission for it to set sail. Your role as a literary captain is to present your manuscript in its finest form, with every page a testament to your dedication and craftsmanship.

Navigate the intricate waters of contracts and royalties, like a captain negotiating favorable terms for the journey ahead. Picture your manuscript as a valuable cargo, and the contract as the maritime agreement that outlines the terms of your literary partnership. Understand the currents of royalties, ensuring a fair distribution of literary treasures as your manuscript sails into the hands of readers.

Understanding Contracts and Royalties: The Literary Negotiator's Dance

As you step onto the literary dance floor of contracts and royalties, envision yourself as a skilled negotiator, gracefully navigating the steps of a negotiation waltz. Understanding contracts and royalties becomes your dance, the artful movement that ensures your interests are represented in the symphony of literary agreements. Think of your manuscript as a dancing partner, and the contract as the choreography that shapes the rhythm of your publishing relationship.

Read contracts with a discerning eye, much like a dancer interpreting the nuances of a complex routine. Imagine your literary journey as a dance, and the contract as the carefully orchestrated steps that guide the flow of your partnership. Your role as a literary negotiator is to ensure that the terms align with your vision, protecting the integrity of your creative expression.

Grasp the intricacies of royalties, like a dancer attuned to the subtle shifts in rhythm and tempo. Picture your manuscript as the centerpiece of the dance floor, and royalties as the beats that echo with each reader's embrace. Understand the financial movements of your literary waltz, ensuring that the rewards are proportionate to the efforts invested in crafting your manuscript.

Chapter 13 Navigator's Log: Literary Coordinates Charted

As we conclude our exploration of the publishing process in Chapter 13, consider this your navigator's log, a guide to charted literary coordinates for your writing journey. Navigating the publishing realm is your North Star, guiding you through the diverse seas of traditional and self-publishing options.

Your readers, like eager passengers, will appreciate the thought and care you invest in steering your manuscript through the publishing waters. Picture your manuscript as a ship under your command, sailing confidently with the wind of your decisions at its back. The literary journey continues, and with a well-navigated publishing process, your writing vessel is poised for an odyssey filled with literary discovery and reader connections.

The Literary Tapestry Unfurls: What Lies Ahead

As we gaze upon the literary tapestry, the journey continues. Chapter 14 awaits, where we dive into the intricacies of marketing your how-to book, a literary endeavor that propels your creation into the hands and hearts of eager readers. The literary threads of your writing journey are being woven, and with each stroke, may your literary masterpiece come closer to fruition. Onward, fellow navigators, to the next chapter in our intricately designed odyssey!

Chapter 14: Marketing Your How-To Book - A Literary Odyssey into Reader Hearts

Greetings, literary trailblazers and marketing maestros! In this chapter of ***"The Author's Manual: Navigating the How-To Writing Process,"*** we embark on a riveting literary odyssey into the enchanting realm of marketing. Imagine this chapter as your literary compass, guiding you through the intricate landscapes of pre-launch preparations, social media exploits, and the delicate art of building relationships that will set your how-to book sailing smoothly into the hearts of eager readers.

Creating a Pre-Launch Marketing Plan: The Literary Strategist's Battle Plan

Envision yourself as a literary strategist, crafting a battle plan that prepares the literary world for the imminent arrival of your masterpiece. Creating a pre-launch marketing plan becomes your strategic playbook, the roadmap that teases and entices potential readers before your book officially sets sail. Picture your manuscript as the flagship of your literary fleet, and the pre-launch marketing plan as the fluttering flag that signals the impending arrival of literary greatness.

Identify your target audience with precision, much like a strategist plotting the optimal course for victory. Imagine your readers as allies waiting to rally behind your literary cause. Craft a pre-launch marketing plan that hones in on the interests and needs of your audience, ensuring that your literary message resonates with the right hearts and minds.

Build anticipation through tantalizing teasers and sneak peeks, like a strategist deploying sneak attacks that keep the opposition guessing. Picture your readers as eager spectators, eagerly awaiting the revelation of your literary arsenal. The literary strategist's battle plan is a carefully calculated sequence of moves that generates a buzz, inviting readers into the anticipatory dance that precedes your book's grand entrance.

Utilizing Social Media, Email, and Other Channels: The Literary Communicator's Symposium

Now, envision yourself as a literary communicator, orchestrating a symposium of messages that echo across the vast expanse of digital landscapes. Utilizing social media, email, and other channels becomes your symposium, the platform where your literary voice reverberates, reaching readers in every corner of the literary realm. Think of your manuscript as a message, and each channel as a different instrument in the symphony of your book's promotion.

Engage with your audience on social media, much like a communicator sparking conversations in a bustling marketplace. Imagine your readers as vibrant participants, contributing to the lively exchange of ideas. Craft posts that not only promote your how-to book but also invite readers into a literary dialogue. The literary communicator's symposium is a space where connections are forged, and your book becomes a topic of enthusiastic discussion.

Leverage the power of email to create a direct line of communication with your readers, reminiscent of a communicator dispatching personalized missives to a loyal following. Picture your readers as recipients eagerly opening literary epistles that carry the essence of your how-to wisdom. Craft emails that go beyond promotion, offering valuable content and fostering a sense of community. The literary communicator's symposium extends beyond the public square, delving into the personal spaces where readers welcome your literary presence.

Explore other channels such as podcasts, interviews, and guest articles, like a communicator taking the stage at various literary gatherings. Imagine your readers as attendees at a literary conference, absorbing the multifaceted facets of your authorial persona. The literary communicator's symposium spans diverse platforms, ensuring that your how-to book resonates with readers who engage with literary content in varied forms.

Building Relationships with Influencers and Reviewers: The Literary Networker's Soirée

As you navigate the social landscape of literary influencers and reviewers, envision yourself as a skilled networker, hosting a soirée that celebrates the power of genuine connections. Building relationships with influencers and reviewers becomes your soirée, the gathering where mutual support and shared literary enthusiasm flourish. Picture your manuscript as the guest of honor, and influencers and reviewers as esteemed attendees who will introduce your work to broader literary circles.

Identify influencers and reviewers whose interests align with your how-to book, much like a networker seeking connections with individuals who resonate with their mission. Imagine your readers as guests at the literary soirée, discovering your book through the endorsements and recommendations of trusted influencers and reviewers. The literary networker's soirée is a collaborative affair, where the combined voices of influencers and reviewers amplify the reach of your literary message.

Approach influencers and reviewers with authenticity, like a networker forming genuine connections based on shared values and interests. Picture your readers as discerning guests, appreciating the sincerity and passion behind the endorsements and reviews. Cultivate relationships that extend beyond the transactional, transforming your literary network into a community of individuals genuinely invested in the success of your how-to book.

Chapter 14 Navigator's Log: Literary Coordinates Aligned

As we conclude our exploration of marketing your how-to book in Chapter 14, consider this your navigator's log, a guide to aligned literary coordinates for your writing journey. Marketing is your North Star, guiding you through the intricate seas of pre-launch preparations, digital symposiums, and networking soirées.

Your readers, like eager attendees, will appreciate the thoughtful and engaging approach you take in introducing them to your literary creation. Picture your manuscript as a celebrated guest, welcomed with open arms into the literary circles that influencers and reviewers navigate. The literary journey continues, and with a well-executed marketing plan, your writing vessel is poised for an odyssey filled with literary resonance and widespread reader connections.

The Literary Tapestry Unfurls: What Lies Ahead

As we gaze upon the literary tapestry, the journey continues. Chapter 15 beckons, where we delve into the nuanced terrain of handling reviews and feedback, a literary landscape that demands resilience and an open heart. The literary threads of your writing journey are being woven, and with each stroke, may your literary masterpiece come closer to fruition. Onward, fellow trailblazers, to the next chapter in our intricately designed odyssey!

Chapter 15: Handling Reviews and Feedback - The Literary Resilience Dance

Salutations, resilient wordsmiths and literary navigators! In this chapter of ***"The Author's Manual: Navigating the How-To Writing Process,"*** we embark on a poignant journey into the nuanced terrain of handling reviews and feedback. Imagine this chapter as your literary sanctuary, a space where the dance of resilience meets the symphony of growth and refinement in the ever-shifting landscape of reader opinions.

Preparing for Both Positive and Constructive Criticism: The Literary Stoic's Posture

Envision yourself as a literary stoic, cultivating a posture of resilience that stands unyielding in the face of both accolades and constructive criticism. Preparing for both positive and constructive criticism becomes your stoic's practice, the art of embracing praise with humility and constructive feedback with an open heart. Picture your manuscript as a resilient dancer, moving gracefully through the literary stage and absorbing the varied rhythms of reader response.

Celebrate positive reviews with gratitude, much like a stoic acknowledging the warmth of sunlight on a literary journey. Imagine your readers as appreciative spectators, expressing admiration for the nuances and wisdom embedded in your how-to book. The literary stoic's posture is one of gratitude, acknowledging the shared joy that comes when your words resonate with readers.

Welcome constructive criticism with an open mind, like a stoic who views challenges as opportunities for growth. Picture your readers as insightful dance partners, offering nuanced perspectives that contribute to the refinement of your literary performance. Embrace feedback as a chance to enhance your craft, recognizing that the dance of resilience is an ongoing evolution of your literary expression.

Strategies for Responding to Feedback: The Literary Diplomat's Art

Now, envision yourself as a literary diplomat, mastering the art of responding to feedback with grace and diplomacy. Strategies for responding to feedback become your diplomatic toolkit, the refined instruments that navigate the delicate exchanges between author and reader. Think of your manuscript as a diplomatic envoy, and each piece of feedback as a diplomatic missive that invites collaboration and understanding.

Express gratitude for positive feedback, much like a diplomat conveying appreciation for a gesture of goodwill. Imagine your readers as diplomatic partners, engaged in a shared journey where appreciation fosters a sense of camaraderie. Craft responses that convey your genuine thanks, creating a literary dialogue that bridges the gap between author and reader.

Approach constructive criticism with a spirit of openness, like a diplomat engaging in a dialogue that seeks common ground. Picture your readers as diplomatic allies, collaborating to enhance the collective literary experience. Respond with humility, acknowledging the validity of diverse perspectives and demonstrating a commitment to continuous improvement in your craft.

Continuous Improvement for Future Editions: The Literary Artisan's Workshop

As you navigate the workshop of continuous improvement, envision yourself as a literary artisan, refining your craft with each stroke of the editorial brush. Continuous improvement for future editions becomes your artisan's endeavor, the commitment to evolving your how-to book into a literary masterpiece that resonates even more deeply with readers. Think of your manuscript as a work of art, and each edition as a canvas where the strokes of refinement contribute to the overall brilliance of your creation.

Analyze patterns in feedback, much like an artisan studying the intricacies of brushstrokes to enhance the visual impact of a painting. Imagine your readers as connoisseurs appreciating the nuances of your literary brushwork. Identify recurring themes in feedback, whether they are areas of praise or constructive suggestions, and use this insight to inform your approach to future editions.

Engage with readers through surveys and polls, like an artisan inviting an audience to share their preferences and insights. Picture your readers as collaborators in the artistic process, contributing to the evolution of your how-to book. Seek their opinions on potential changes or enhancements, ensuring that the continuous improvement of your literary creation is a collective endeavor.

Chapter 15 Navigator's Log: Literary Coordinates Recalibrated

As we conclude our exploration of handling reviews and feedback in Chapter 15, consider this your navigator's log, a guide to recalibrated literary coordinates for your writing journey. Resilience is your North Star, guiding you through the intricate seas of reader opinions, both uplifting and constructive.

Your readers, like dance partners in the literary ballroom, will appreciate the resilience and grace with which you navigate the nuanced terrain of feedback. Picture your manuscript as a masterpiece in progress, evolving with each step in the dance of continuous improvement. The literary journey continues, and with a resilient response to reviews and feedback, your writing vessel is poised for an odyssey filled with refined artistry and a deeper connection with your audience.

The Literary Tapestry Unfurls: What Lies Ahead

As we gaze upon the literary tapestry, the journey continues. Chapter 16 awaits, where we dive into the role of technology in how-to writing, a literary exploration that embraces the tools and trends shaping the modern landscape of authorship. The literary threads of your writing journey are being woven, and with each stroke, may your literary masterpiece come closer to fruition. Onward, fellow wordsmiths, to the next chapter in our intricately designed odyssey!

Chapter 16: Leveraging Technology in How-To Writing - A Literary Symphony of Innovation

Greetings, literary pioneers and tech-savvy wordsmiths! In this chapter of ***"The Author's Manual: Navigating the How-To Writing Process,"*** we embark on a captivating exploration into the symbiotic relationship between literature and technology. Picture this chapter as your literary laboratory, where the alchemy of words converges with the magic of modern tools, shaping your how-to book into a literary masterpiece that resonates with the pulse of the digital age.

Utilizing Writing Tools and Software: The Literary Alchemist's Arsenal

Envision yourself as a literary alchemist, armed with a digital arsenal that enhances the alchemy of your words into literary gold. Utilizing writing tools and software becomes your alchemist's craft, the meticulous blend of traditional storytelling with the innovation of modern technology. Imagine your manuscript as a potion, and each writing tool and software as an essential ingredient that transforms your narrative into a literary elixir.

Explore word processing software with the curiosity of an alchemist delving into ancient manuscripts. Picture your readers as seekers of literary wisdom, yearning to absorb the clarity and elegance that technology brings to your prose. Experiment with features that streamline your writing process, allowing you to focus on the artistry of your words rather than the mechanics of formatting.

Harness the power of grammar and style-checking tools, like an alchemist refining the purity of precious metals. Imagine your readers as connoisseurs of literary craftsmanship, appreciating the polished and error-free composition of your how-to book. Use these tools to ensure that your prose sparkles with literary brilliance, free from the distractions of grammatical missteps.

Exploring Multimedia Options for Enhanced Content: The Literary Visionary's Canvas

Now, envision yourself as a literary visionary, painting a vivid canvas where words blend seamlessly with multimedia elements. Exploring multimedia options for enhanced content becomes your visionary palette, the artistic fusion of text, images, and interactive elements that captivates your readers in a sensory symphony. Think of your manuscript as a multimedia masterpiece, and each element as a brushstroke that adds depth and richness to your literary composition.

Incorporate images, diagrams, and charts with the finesse of a visionary curator arranging an art exhibit. Picture your readers as gallery visitors, appreciating the visual feast that complements and elucidates your how-to instructions. Select visuals that amplify the clarity of your content, turning each page into a canvas that engages both the mind and the eye.

Collaborate with designers and illustrators, like a visionary orchestrating a symphony with a team of skilled musicians. Imagine your readers as audience members, enjoying a collaborative performance where the visual elements harmonize seamlessly with your written narrative. Work closely with your artistic collaborators to ensure that every visual component enhances the literary experience, transforming your how-to book into a work of multidimensional art.

Staying Current with Industry Trends: The Literary Trendsetter's Pulse

As you navigate the ever-evolving landscape of literary technology, envision yourself as a trendsetter, attuned to the pulse of innovation shaping the modern authorial journey. Staying current with industry trends becomes your trendsetter's rhythm, the ongoing dance with the latest advancements that infuse your how-to book with a literary heartbeat. Think of your manuscript as a living entity, and staying current with industry trends as the vitality that ensures its relevance in a dynamic literary ecosystem.

Embrace the rise of augmented reality (AR) and virtual reality (VR) technologies, like a trendsetter incorporating avant-garde elements into a traditional art form. Picture your readers as literary adventurers, immersing themselves in an interactive experience where your words come to life in a virtual realm. Experiment with the possibilities that AR and VR offer, elevating your how-to book into a literary adventure that transcends the boundaries of traditional storytelling.

Consider the potential of interactive e-books, envisioning your manuscript as a choose-your-own-adventure literary journey. Imagine your readers as active participants, navigating through your how-to instructions in a personalized and engaging manner. Embrace the interactivity that technology affords, transforming your how-to book into a literary playground where readers become co-creators of their learning experience.

Chapter 16 Navigator's Log: Literary Coordinates Illuminated

As we conclude our exploration of leveraging technology in how-to writing in Chapter 16, consider this your navigator's log, a guide to illuminated literary coordinates for your writing journey. Technology is your North Star, guiding you through the intricate seas of writing tools, multimedia exploration, and industry trends.

Your readers, like literary companions on a digital odyssey, will appreciate the thoughtful integration of technology that enhances their reading experience. Picture your manuscript as a technological marvel, seamlessly blending the artistry of words with the innovation of the digital age. The literary journey continues, and with a well-leveraged arsenal of technology, your writing vessel is poised for an odyssey filled with literary innovation and reader engagement.

The Literary Tapestry Unfurls: What Lies Ahead

As we gaze upon the literary tapestry, the journey continues. Chapter 17 beckons, where we delve into the legal and ethical considerations of how-to writing, a literary exploration that navigates the delicate balance between creativity and responsibility. The literary threads of your writing journey are being woven, and with each stroke, may your literary masterpiece come closer to fruition. Onward, fellow wordsmiths, to the next chapter in our intricately designed odyssey!

Chapter 17: Legal and Ethical Considerations - Navigating the Literary Seas with Integrity

Ahoy, literary captains and guardians of ethical shores! In this chapter ***of "The Author's Manual: Navigating the How-To Writing Process,"*** we set sail into the intricate waters of legal and ethical considerations in the expansive realm of literary creation. Picture this chapter as your ethical compass, ensuring that your literary voyage is not only creatively fulfilling but also sails the seas of authorship with the winds of integrity.

Copyright Issues in Literary Seas: Safeguarding Your Creative Ship

Envision yourself as a vigilant guardian, safeguarding your creative ship from the storms of copyright issues that may lurk in the literary seas. Copyright issues become your watchtower, the elevated vantage point from which you survey the legal horizons, protecting your literary creation from unwarranted challenges. Picture your manuscript as a treasure chest of originality, and copyright as the key that preserves its sanctity in the vast literary ocean.

Understand the nuances of fair use, much like a vigilant guardian deciphering the permissible boundaries of literary borrowing. Imagine your readers as fellow sailors, navigating the literary sea with a shared understanding of the principles that uphold ethical use of intellectual property. Educate yourself on fair use guidelines, ensuring that your how-to book respects the rights of other creators while maintaining the authenticity of your voice.

Navigate the realm of public domain with the prudence of a seasoned navigator exploring charted territories. Picture your readers as explorers in the literary landscape, benefitting from the wealth of public domain knowledge that enriches your how-to book. Acknowledge the boundaries of public domain and exercise caution to avoid legal entanglements, ensuring that your literary vessel sails smoothly through the open waters of shared knowledge.

Avoiding Plagiarism and Respecting Intellectual Property: The Literary Steward's Creed

Now, envision yourself as a literary steward, embracing a creed that venerates the principles of originality and intellectual property. Avoiding plagiarism and respecting intellectual property becomes your steward's pledge, the solemn vow that protects your how-to book from the ethical pitfalls of literary theft. Think of your manuscript as a literary sanctuary, and each idea within it as a cherished artifact that deserves acknowledgment and protection.

Cite sources with the diligence of a meticulous archivist cataloging the treasures within a library. Imagine your readers as scholars, valuing the transparency and integrity that proper citation brings to your how-to book. Embed a culture of citation in your writing, acknowledging the intellectual contributions of others and fortifying the foundation of your literary creation with the strength of ethical sourcing.

Steer clear of unintentional plagiarism with the mindfulness of a conscientious sailor avoiding hidden rocks in literary waters. Picture your readers as fellow navigators, trusting in the authenticity of your words and ideas. Utilize plagiarism detection tools to ensure that your manuscript remains untarnished by unintentional replication, maintaining the literary integrity of your work.

Ethical Considerations in Content Creation: The Literary Guardian's Oath

As you traverse the literary seas, envision yourself as a literary guardian, upholding an oath that prioritizes ethical considerations in content creation. Ethical considerations become your guiding beacon, the moral compass that illuminates the path toward responsible authorship. Imagine your manuscript as a beacon of ethical excellence, radiating principles that resonate with readers and fellow authors alike.

Navigate the delicate terrain of sensitive topics with empathy, much like a compassionate guardian steering clear of tumultuous waters. Picture your readers as passengers on a literary journey, trusting in your ethical navigation through potentially contentious subjects. Approach sensitive topics with sensitivity and mindfulness, fostering a safe and respectful environment within your how-to book.

Consider the diversity of perspectives in your literary crew, envisioning your readers as a vibrant community of individuals with varied beliefs and backgrounds. Embrace inclusivity and fairness in your content, acknowledging the richness that different voices bring to the literary conversation. Strive to create a how-to book that welcomes readers from all walks of life, fostering a sense of belonging within the literary community you've cultivated.

Chapter 17 Navigator's Log: Literary Coordinates Anchored in Integrity

As we conclude our exploration of legal and ethical considerations in Chapter 17, consider this your navigator's log, a guide to anchored literary coordinates for your writing journey. Integrity is your North Star, guiding you through the intricate seas of copyright, plagiarism, and ethical content creation.

Your readers, like ethical allies on a literary quest, will appreciate the conscientious approach you take in safeguarding the integrity of your work. Picture your manuscript as a testament to ethical authorship, a how-to book that not only imparts knowledge but also stands as a beacon of responsible and principled creation. The literary journey continues, and with a commitment to legal and ethical considerations, your writing vessel is poised for an odyssey filled with ethical authorship and a flourishing literary community.

The Literary Tapestry Unfurls: What Lies Ahead

As we gaze upon the literary tapestry, the journey continues. Chapter 18 awaits, where we delve into the intricate landscape of crafting effective titles and subtitles, a literary exploration that combines the art of creativity with the science of marketability. The literary threads of your writing journey are being woven, and with each stroke, may your literary masterpiece come closer to fruition. Onward, fellow stewards of the written word, to the next chapter in our intricately designed odyssey!

Chapter 18: Crafting Effective Titles and Subtitles - The Literary Alchemy of Creativity and Marketability

Salutations, literary architects and title maestros! In this chapter of ***"The Author's Manual: Navigating the How-To Writing Process,"*** we embark on a thrilling exploration into the art and science of crafting effective titles and subtitles. Imagine this chapter as your literary workshop, where the alchemy of creativity and marketability converges, birthing a title that not only resonates with the soul but also beckons readers with a magnetic charm.

Importance of a Compelling Title: The Literary Overture to Your Masterpiece

Envision yourself as a master composer, creating the overture to your literary masterpiece with a compelling title. The importance of a compelling title becomes your symphonic prelude, the resonant notes that echo through the literary corridors, inviting readers to immerse themselves in the orchestration of your how-to book. Picture your manuscript as a grand performance, and the title as the crescendo that captivates attention and sets the stage for the narrative journey within.

Understand the role of the title as the literary ambassador of your work, much like a seasoned diplomat representing the essence of a nation. Imagine your readers as curious citizens of the literary realm, drawn to your book by the allure of a well-crafted title. Craft a title that encapsulates the spirit of your how-to book, offering readers a glimpse into the literary landscape they are about to traverse.

Consider the resonance of your title in the literary marketplace, envisioning it as a beacon that guides readers amid the vast sea of book options. Picture your readers as navigators seeking a literary destination, relying on your title as a compass that directs them toward your how-to book. Strive for a title that not only reflects the content but also aligns with the expectations and interests of your target audience.

Creating Subtitles that Clarify and Entice: The Literary Art of Elucidation

Now, envision yourself as a literary illuminator, using subtitles as the brushstrokes that clarify and entice, much like an artist accentuating the nuances of a painting. Creating subtitles that clarify and entice becomes your artful expression, the nuanced dance of words that guides readers through the intricate terrain of your how-to book while enticing them with the promise of valuable insights. Think of your manuscript as a canvas, and the subtitle as the brush that adds layers of meaning to your literary creation.

Craft subtitles that provide a roadmap for readers, much like a skilled guide offering clear directions through uncharted territories. Imagine your readers as intrepid explorers, relying on your subtitle to navigate the literary landscape you've crafted. Ensure that your subtitle offers a concise yet comprehensive preview of what readers can expect, making it an indispensable companion to the title.

Infuse a sense of intrigue into your subtitle, envisioning it as a literary teaser that sparks curiosity. Picture your readers as eager participants in a literary adventure, enticed by the prospect of uncovering valuable knowledge within your how-to book. Strike a balance between clarity and allure, creating a subtitle that not only informs but also captivates, compelling readers to delve deeper into the literary journey you've meticulously prepared.

Considering Marketability and SEO: The Literary Strategist's Playbook

As you navigate the realm of crafting titles and subtitles, envision yourself as a literary strategist, wielding a playbook that considers marketability and SEO as essential tactics. Considering marketability and SEO becomes your strategic compass, the guide that ensures your how-to book not only captures the literary essence but also sails smoothly through the digital currents of online discoverability. Imagine your manuscript as a literary voyage, and marketability and SEO as the favorable winds that propel it toward a wider readership.

Research keywords relevant to your how-to book, much like a seasoned navigator plotting the course based on celestial landmarks. Picture your readers as digital wayfarers, using search engines as their compass in the vast expanse of online literature. Infuse strategic keywords into your title and subtitle, enhancing the discoverability of your how-to book and ensuring it stands out in the literary constellation.

Consider the market trends and reader preferences in your genre, envisioning them as currents that influence the trajectory of your literary vessel. Picture your readers as enthusiasts navigating literary waters, drawn to books that align with their current interests. Align your title and subtitle with prevailing trends, ensuring that your how-to book becomes a literary beacon that captures the attention of readers exploring the literary marketplace.

Chapter 18 Navigator's Log: Literary Coordinates Aligned for Impact

As we conclude our exploration of crafting effective titles and subtitles in Chapter 18, consider this your navigator's log, a guide to aligned literary coordinates for your writing journey. The alchemy of creativity, marketability, and SEO is your North Star, guiding you through the intricate seas of title and subtitle creation.

Your readers, like literary passengers on a captivating voyage, will appreciate the thoughtful craftsmanship you bring to the creation of your title and subtitle. Picture your manuscript as a literary masterpiece, and the title as its crown jewel that not only reflects the brilliance within but also beckons readers to discover its treasures. The literary journey continues, and with a well-crafted title and subtitle, your writing vessel is poised for an odyssey filled with reader engagement and literary impact.

The Literary Tapestry Unfurls: What Lies Ahead

As we gaze upon the literary tapestry, the journey continues. Chapter 19 awaits, where we explore the art of building a community around your book, a literary endeavor that transforms readers into a thriving community of enthusiasts. The literary threads of your writing journey are being woven, and with each stroke, may your literary masterpiece come closer to fruition. Onward, fellow literary artisans, to the next chapter in our

Chapter 19: Building a Community Around Your Book - The Literary Tapestry of Connection and Belonging

Greetings, literary architects and community builders! In this chapter of *"The Author's Manual: Navigating the How-To Writing Process,"* we embark on a splendid exploration into the art of building a community around your book. Picture this chapter as your literary workshop, where the threads of connection and belonging are intricately woven into the fabric of your how-to masterpiece. Imagine your manuscript not just as a solitary creation but as the catalyst for a vibrant community of enthusiasts bound together by a shared literary passion.

Engaging with Readers through Forums and Social Media: The Literary Town Square

Envision yourself as the mayor of a bustling literary town, engaging with readers through forums and social media as the lively town square where ideas are exchanged and connections flourish. Engaging with readers becomes your mayoral duty, the active participation that transforms your how-to book from a static creation into a dynamic hub of literary discourse. Picture your manuscript as the centerpiece of this literary town, and readers as the vibrant townsfolk gathering to share insights and stories.

Explore online forums and groups related to your how-to book's genre, much like a mayor engaging with diverse communities within the town. Imagine your readers as citizens with varied interests and backgrounds, each contributing a unique perspective to the literary conversation. Actively participate in these digital town squares, fostering a sense of camaraderie and encouraging readers to share their experiences and questions related to your how-to book.

Harness the power of social media platforms, envisioning them as the lively streets where literary discussions and celebrations unfold. Picture your readers as parade participants, joining the festive procession of tweets, posts, and comments that celebrate the essence of your how-to book. Leverage social media to share valuable content, host interactive discussions, and connect with readers on a personal level, transforming your how-to book into a literary beacon in the digital landscape.

Hosting Workshops and Webinars: The Literary Symposium

Now, envision yourself as the curator of a literary symposium, hosting workshops and webinars that bring readers together in a collaborative exploration of your how-to book. Hosting workshops and webinars becomes your curatorial craft, the artful arrangement of interactive sessions that elevate the reader's experience beyond the pages of your manuscript. Think of your how-to book as the central theme of this literary symposium, and readers as eager participants seeking to delve deeper into the knowledge you've shared.

Design workshops that allow readers to actively apply the principles from your how-to book, much like a curator organizing hands-on activities in an art exhibit. Imagine your readers as apprentices, refining their skills and gaining practical insights through interactive sessions. Foster a sense of shared learning, where participants contribute their experiences and perspectives, enriching the collective knowledge of the literary symposium.

Conduct webinars that provide a virtual stage for in-depth discussions and Q&A sessions, envisioning them as the auditorium where readers can connect with you in real-time. Picture your readers as audience members, eager to engage with the author behind the words and explore the nuances of your how-to book. Use webinars to share behind-the-scenes anecdotes, answer questions, and forge a personal connection with your literary community, creating a sense of intimacy in the vast literary auditorium.

Creating a Lasting Connection with Your Audience: The Literary Fellowship

As you navigate the landscape of building a community around your book, envision yourself as the architect of a lasting literary fellowship—a space where readers feel a sense of belonging and connection. Creating a lasting connection with your audience becomes your architectural endeavor, the intentional design that transforms casual readers into dedicated members of your literary fellowship. Imagine your how-to book not as a standalone creation but as the cornerstone of this literary fellowship, and readers as cherished members contributing to its vibrancy.

Establish a dedicated author website or blog, envisioning it as the headquarters of your literary fellowship, a place where readers can gather, explore additional content, and stay updated on your literary journey. Picture your readers as visitors to a literary sanctuary, seeking not only the wisdom within your how-to book but also the ongoing narrative of your authorial adventure. Share articles, insights, and updates, inviting readers to become active participants in the evolving story of your literary fellowship.

Create a newsletter that serves as a personalized letter to your literary community, much like a correspondence between friends sharing news and reflections. Imagine your readers as pen pals, eagerly awaiting each newsletter as a window into the author's world and the latest developments in the literary fellowship. Use the newsletter to cultivate a sense of intimacy, express gratitude, and provide exclusive content that deepens the connection between you and your readers.

Chapter 19 Navigator's Log: Literary Coordinates Anchored in Connection

As we conclude our exploration of building a community around your book in Chapter 19, consider this your navigator's log—a guide to anchored literary coordinates for your writing journey. Connection and belonging are your North Star, guiding you through the intricate seas of reader engagement and community building.

Your readers, like cherished companions on a literary quest, will appreciate the intentional efforts you invest in building a community around your how-to book. Picture your manuscript not only as a source of knowledge but also as the catalyst for lasting connections and shared experiences. The literary journey continues, and with a thriving literary fellowship, your writing vessel is poised for an odyssey filled with meaningful connections and the collective celebration of literary passion.

The Literary Tapestry Unfurls: What Lies Ahead

As we gaze upon the literary tapestry, the journey continues. Chapter 20 beckons, where we reflect on the author's journey, celebrating successes, learning from challenges, and offering encouragement for the ongoing odyssey. The literary threads of your writing journey are being woven, and with each stroke, may your literary masterpiece come closer to fruition. Onward, fellow architects of literary worlds, to the next chapter in our intricately designed odyssey!

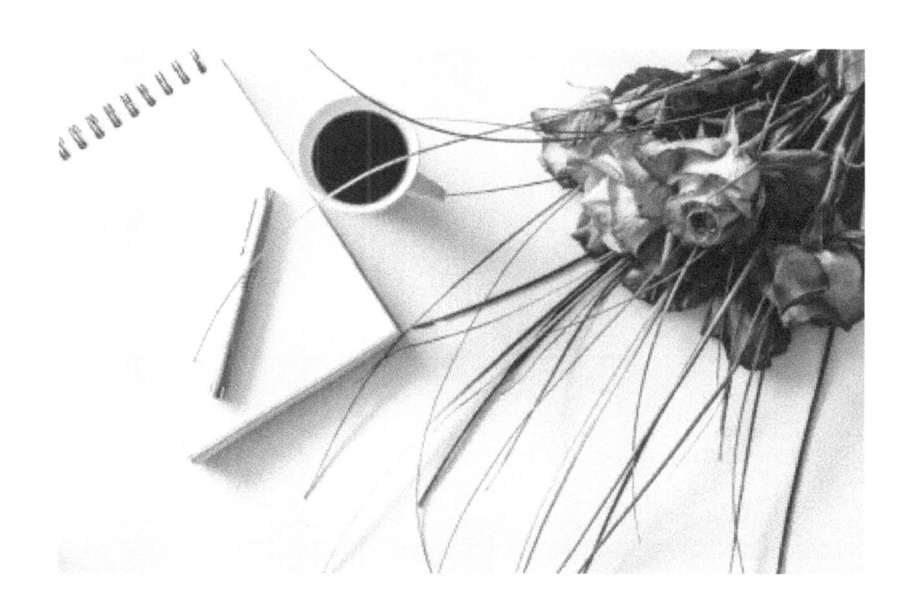

Chapter 20: The Author's Journey Continues - Reflections, Celebrations, and Literary Encouragement

Greetings, fellow literary sojourners, as we step into the final chapter of *"The Author's Manual: Navigating the How-To Writing Process."* This chapter serves as a literary reflection, a celebration of triumphs, an acknowledgment of challenges, and a heartfelt encouragement for the ongoing odyssey that is the author's journey. Picture this chapter as a literary fireplace, where we gather to share stories, offer insights, and bask in the warmth of the literary community we've cultivated.

Reflection on the Writing Process: The Literary Tapestry Unveiled

Envision yourself as the curator of a grand literary exhibit, reflecting on the intricate tapestry of your writing process. Reflection on the writing process becomes your curator's stroll, the leisurely exploration through the corridors of creativity, revisiting the milestones, and marveling at the nuances woven into the fabric of your how-to book. Picture your manuscript as the centerpiece of this literary exhibit, and each chapter as a vibrant thread contributing to the rich tapestry of your authorial journey.

Reflect on the evolution of your ideas from sparks of inspiration to fully-fledged chapters, much like a curator observing the transformation of raw materials into a masterpiece. Imagine your readers as museum visitors, appreciating the journey each idea took to become a part of your how-to book. Embrace the fluctuations in your creative process, acknowledging the ebb and flow of inspiration, and celebrate the resilience that brought your literary vision to fruition.

Consider the growth you've experienced as an author throughout the writing journey, envisioning it as the maturation of an artist honing their craft. Picture your readers as connoisseurs of literary art, recognizing the refinement in your writing style, the deepening of your insights, and the mastery gained through the challenges overcome. Embrace the continuous evolution of your authorial identity, knowing that each stroke of the pen contributes to the ever-expanding canvas of your literary legacy.

Celebrating Successes and Learning from Challenges: The Literary Festival of Experience

Now, imagine yourself as the organizer of a grand literary festival, celebrating successes and learning from challenges as the collective experience that enriches the author's journey. Celebrating successes and learning from challenges becomes your festival planning, the meticulous orchestration of events that recognize achievements and distill lessons from the trials faced. Think of your how-to book as the star attraction of this literary festival, and your readers as participants in the collective celebration of authorship.

Celebrate the completion of your manuscript as a literary victory, much like a festival finale that culminates in a dazzling display of fireworks. Picture your readers as festival goers, applauding the dedication and perseverance that led to the creation of your how-to book. Acknowledge the triumph of reaching the final chapter, savoring the sense of accomplishment, and revel in the applause of a literary audience appreciating the fruits of your labor.

Leverage challenges as stepping stones toward growth, envisioning them as the unexpected plot twists that add depth to the author's narrative. Imagine your readers as fellow travelers on the literary path, each facing their unique challenges and deriving inspiration from your journey. Share the lessons learned from navigating setbacks, embracing the imperfections, and transforming obstacles into opportunities for literary exploration.

Encouragement for the Ongoing Literary Odyssey: The Literary Torch Passed On

As you stand at the threshold of the final chapter, envision yourself as a torchbearer passing on the flame of encouragement for the ongoing literary odyssey. Encouragement for the ongoing literary odyssey becomes your torchbearer's pledge—the commitment to illuminate the path for aspiring authors following in your literary footsteps. Picture your readers as torchbearers in training, ready to embark on their own journeys, fueled by the flame of your insights and encouragement.

Offer words of wisdom to authors setting sail on their writing adventures, much like a seasoned guide sharing navigational tips for the literary seas. Imagine your readers as fledgling authors, absorbing the encouragement to persevere through challenges, trust in their unique voice, and revel in the joy of connecting with readers. Share the truth that the author's journey is a continual odyssey, and each step, whether smooth or challenging, contributes to the rich narrative of a literary legacy.

Express gratitude for the literary community that has formed around your how-to book, envisioning it as a shared campfire where authors gather to exchange stories and support one another. Picture your readers as fellow campers, drawn together by a shared passion for the written word. Cultivate a spirit of camaraderie, encouraging authors to celebrate each other's successes, offer solace during challenges, and collectively elevate the literary landscape.

Chapter 20 Navigator's Log: Literary Coordinates Anchored in Reflection and Hope

As we conclude our exploration in the final chapter, consider this your navigator's log, a guide to anchored literary coordinates for the ongoing journey. Reflection, celebration, and encouragement are your North Star, guiding you and your readers through the intricate seas of the author's journey.

Your readers, like kindred spirits around the literary campfire, will appreciate the insights and encouragement you've shared. Picture your manuscript not as a solitary creation but as a catalyst for a community of authors supporting one another. The literary journey continues, and with reflections, celebrations, and encouragement, your writing vessel is poised for an odyssey filled with ongoing growth, connection, and the perpetual magic of storytelling.

The Literary Tapestry Unfurls: What Lies Ahead

As we gaze upon the literary tapestry, the journey continues. While this chapter marks the end of ***"The Author's Manual,"*** the narrative of your authorial journey is far from over. The threads of your writing adventure are being woven into the fabric of literary history, and with each stroke, may your literary masterpiece continue to inspire, resonate, and contribute to the ever-expanding narrative of the written word. Onward, fellow torchbearers of storytelling, to the next chapter in our intricately designed odyssey!

Don't miss out!

Visit the website below and you can sign up to receive emails whenever Richard D. Krause publishes a new book. There's no charge and no obligation.

https://books2read.com/r/B-A-HQUAB-YAPQC

BOOKS 2 READ

Connecting independent readers to independent writers.

Did you love *The Author's Manual: Navigating the How-To Writing Process*? Then you should read *From Words To Wealth: Mastering Freelance Writing*[1] by Richard Krause!

2

In the digital age, the power of words has taken on a new significance. In a world where information is king, those who wield the pen skillfully hold the keys to success. Welcome to "From Words to Wealth: Mastering Freelance Writing," your definitive guide to embarking on a journey that offers not just financial prosperity but the freedom to chart your own course.

Freelance writing is more than a profession; it's a gateway to unlimited opportunities. It's the art of transforming thoughts into words and words into wealth. Whether you're a budding wordsmith, a seasoned scribe, or someone simply intrigued by the idea of writing

1. https://books2read.com/u/bxBk26

2. https://books2read.com/u/bxBk26

your way to financial freedom, this ebook is your passport to a realm where creativity meets prosperity.

We'll navigate the labyrinthine world of freelance writing together, uncovering the secrets to success that will empower you to:

Discover your writing passion and unique voice.

Master the essential writing skills that captivate audiences.

Build a thriving freelance writing career from the comfort of your own home.

Negotiate contracts and set rates that reflect your true worth.

Create a compelling writer's portfolio that opens doors to high-paying projects.

Forge lasting client relationships through effective communication and professionalism.

Navigate the ethical and legal nuances of freelance writing.

Diversify your income streams and expand your freelance business.

Find inspiration and overcome the challenges that every freelancer faces.

Embrace the future trends that will shape the freelance writing industry.

Join us on this exciting journey as we unveil the strategies, tips, and insights that will transform your words into wealth. Whether you're driven by the dream of financial independence or the love of the written word, "From Words to Wealth" is your guidebook to mastering freelance writing and crafting a life of both prosperity and creative fulfillment.

Are you ready to embark on your path to pen, profit, and freedom? Let's begin.

Read more at https://rkrause45.wixsite.com/mysite.

Also by Richard D. Krause

The Elderly Trap: Uncovering Scams and Reclaiming Security in the Golden Years.
Ignite Your Motivation and Achieve Your Dreams
The Art of Persoal Mastery: A Roadmap to Success and Fulfillment
The Serenity Solution: Mastering Happiness through Meditation
The Spice Cabinet Apothecary: Natural Health at Your Fingertips
The Author's Manual: Navigating the How-To Writing Process

Milton Keynes UK
Ingram Content Group UK Ltd.
UKHW020246221123
432980UK00016B/966